PREFACE

This ebook is meant to educate you on blockchain and cryptocurrency, it dives dip into the key factors that crypto traders use to evaluate a project and much beneficial information that will help you stay profitable in the space. This book is meant to help you develop a profitable trading strategy. Please note that this book cannot be seen as financial advice but should serve educational purposes only. Those who wish to practice what is written in this book do so with the understanding that trading is risky.

Title: One Trade Per Day

Author: AUSTIN AMADI

Release Date: July 24, 2022

Language: English

TABLE OF CONTENTS

INTRODUCTION

Trading cryptocurrency has made millionaires and also sent people parking, at this time cryptocurrency does not have regulations like the mainstream financial markets, even the mainstream markets with all their regulations have fraud and scams. What does cryptocurrency stand for, is it effective, and is it making the much-requested change we want in the financial system of the world?Is cryptocurrency perfect or the new haven for criminals and gullible people? To me, cryptocurrency is the now and future of money and is disrupting the way we transact, and anything that changes the traditional way or a way people are accustomed to must face setbacks from those who are already benefiting from the state of things. Blockchain technology is the future and is solving the problem of trust which is the greatest issue of the 21st century. Trust has been one issue the world has not looked into, the rise of chaos, wars, and confrontation between countries all these points to the lack of trust that discredits agreements and treaties. Blockchain technology is helping people transact border less, trust less and in a secured traceable transaction, this exactly is the solution that is much needed. Learning about blockchain at this time is positioning yourself for a future that must come when everyone will envy the early adopters of this technology. We are lucky to be part of this revolution and you are welcome to spread the information everywhere and anywhere. Blockchain and Cryptocurrency is here to stay!

FOR YOUR OWN GOOD

Emotional Intelligence

An experience they say is the best teacher, but for those who live to tell the tale. A bad experience always creates fear and people never return to what they fear. Before you start trading are you Emotionally Strong to handle losses? need I remind you that every good trader loses money from time to time? Emotional Intelligence is your ability to handle your emotions and those people around you. Your understanding is that there is a 50% chance you can lose your money so you must be prepared.

Patience

One of the qualities you must master is patience because sometimes the best thing to do is to do nothing, you must learn to stick to the plan. One of the reasons people lose money is not sticking to their strategy, they spend time developing strategies they don't use. Stick to the initial plan.

Overtrading

Over-trading is not good for you, set a target for yourself and when you meet that target leave the market, just go and rest. Be calm and calculated, you are a professional, allow those making billions to make, the whole idea is to make money and not lose it. In this market any day you don't lose money, you have won! even if you didn't make at all.

Chase knowledge

The biggest mistake beginners make, is to believe they can become professionals after watching a few youtube videos. Everything worthwhile Is uphill. Trading is a profession, like every other profession it requires skills and these skills are not developed in a day. Trading is a risky profession and hence requires an even greater skill set to succeed. You must be cautious to learn as much as possible before starting, you must learn the behaviour of coins, market cycles and factors that influence the market.

Do not trade money you need for groceries

It is a bad idea to do this because it puts too much pressure on you and that will affect your decisions and increase your greed. Only use the money you don't need soon and you can afford to lose.

Think Long Term

Hodlers will always win, trading is not getting rich quick, but getting rich sure. Think about trading as an investment you need to watch grow. If you stay long enough in the environment you will enjoy the dividend of your efforts.

Chapter I

INTRODUCTION TO BLOCKCHAIN

What is blockchain?

A blockchain is a digital ledger of transactions distributed across the entire network of computer systems. Each block in the chain contains several transactions, and every time a new transaction occurs on the blockchain, a record of that transaction is added to every participant's ledger. Instead of storing records on one computer, it is shared amongst many computers on the network, with this each computer on the network holds a record of the transaction making it very secure and immutable. Currently, there are at least four types of blockchain networks such as public blockchains, private blockchains, consortium blockchains and hybrid blockchains.

A Block

A block is a group of data within a blockchain. On blockchains, blocks are made up of transaction records as users buy or sell coins. Each block can hold only a certain amount of information, once it reaches that limit a new block is formed to continue the chain.

Genesis Block

The first block of a cryptocurrency ever mined.

Halving

A feature written into Bitcoin's code in which after a certain number of blocks are mined (typically every four years) the amount of new Bitcoin entering circulation gets halved. The halving can have an impact on Bitcoin's price.

Hash

A unique string of numbers and letters that identify blocks and are tied to crypto buyers and sellers.

FEATURES OF BLOCKCHAIN TECHNOLOGY

Programmable

The technology can be modified to suit any field of work. Using smart contracts you can further programme certain conditions that should be met before a transaction is executed this ensures that both parties keep their part of the bargain.

Immutable

With blockchain records cant be falsified, once the transaction is successful no one can delete the record or make changes to it. This prevents discrepancies and transactions can't be reversed.

Timestamped

Transactions on the blockchain are time stamped, i.e the transactions have a time of execution which can be seen on the transaction details as proof to authenticate the transaction.

Distributed

All participants of the network have a copy of the records making this even more impossible to alter the records because that means you will have to change them on all participant's networks.

Security

All the transactions done on a blockchain are individually encrypted making every transaction unique.

Unanimous

Everyone must agree that a transaction is valid before it is carried out, so there is always unity in the agreement of each individual record.

Anonymity

The identity of the participants is not revealed, anyone, anywhere, any race can participate as far as they are connected to the internet.

If the internet changed the way we interact, blockchain is changing the way we transact.

INTRODUCTION TO CRYPTOCURRENCIES

One of the uses of Blockchain is cryptocurrency, which is a daughter of blockchain technology. Let me add that Blockchain was already in existence before cryptocurrency.
Cryptocurrency is any form of currency that exists digitally or virtually and uses cryptography to secure transactions.

Cryptocurrency allows the transfer of value between peers without the need for a central authority.

Bitcoin

This is a digital or virtual currency that operates outside the influence of a person or group of persons, this is the breakthrough product that has led to the invention of other cryptocurrencies, as such Bitcoin is considered the king of all currencies and values as gold. *Any cryptocurrency other than bitcoin is called an altcoin.*

Ethereum

According to the Ethereum website: *https://ethereum.org/en/* Ethereum is a technology that's home to digital money, global payments, and applications. The community has built a booming digital economy, bold new ways for creators to earn online, and so much more. It's open to everyone, wherever you are in the world – all you need is the internet.

Binance

In 2017, Binance and BNB were born. Three years later, Binance Smart Chain (BSC) was introduced to the world.

As Binance grew bigger and stronger, so did Binance Smart Chain. BSC was born in time for the Defi revolution, as the public showed increased interest in alternative financial solutions and use cases powered by blockchain. Today, both Binance and BSC remain connected by BNB. *copied from https://www.binance.com/en/blog/*

Stablecoin or Digital Fiat

A stablecoin is pegged to a non-digital asset or currency, this can also be referred to as digital fiat. An example is USDT which is pegged to the US dollar.

There are more than 1900 cryptocurrencies in existence and many more are on the way, many blockchain infrastructures are being built daily in the interest of all. A good number of these blockchains and cryptocurrencies leverage the Ethereum blockchain.

Coin and Tokens

There are basically not many differences between a *Coin and a Token,* crypto coins are the native asset of a Blockchain like Bitcoin or Ethereum, whereas crypto tokens are created by platforms and applications that are built on top of an existing Blockchain.

Fork

When the community of a particular blockchain decides to make changes to the blockchain's protocol, a fork is created which has similarities to the old blockchain and changes to the protocol.

Bitcoin Cash is a fork of Bitcoin.

WALLETS

Crypto wallets are used to access your digital assets on the blockchain.

Crypto assets do not actually hold your assets but hold the keys which help you assess your assets on the blockchain. Your key is proof of ownership of the asset on the blockchain and it is accessed through a crypto wallet.

Hot Wallets

Hot wallets store your Digital assets online. Some online wallets are exchanges and other wallets. Hot wallets are divided into custodial and non-custodial wallets.

Custodial wallets

This kind of wallet needs you to register on the platform and anytime you want to log in you need a username and password. The platform handles this kind of wallet's security and you do not have total custody of the wallet's security.

Custodial wallets are mostly on exchanges and trading platforms so anything that happens to the exchange will surely affect your wallet.

It is less safe compared to other wallets.

Non Custodial Wallets

This kind of wallet gives you access to your security key, meaning that there can only be one access to the wallet which is by importing the keys into the wallet.

it is considered more secure but one must be careful not to lose the security keys or phrases. *No key No wallet.*

Hardware Wallets

A Hardware wallet or cold wallet allows you to store your assets offline, which is surely the safest way to store your assets.

With hardware wallets, your asset is stored in hardware and uses a physical medium. Some examples of hardware wallets include

Ledger Nano S, Trezor Model One- Crypto Hardware Wallet and SafePal S1.

Paper Wallets

Keys are written on a physical medium like paper and stored in a safe place. This of course makes using your crypto harder because as digital money it can only be used on the internet.

When choosing a wallet to use, security should be the most important thing to consider. When using a non custodial wallet always write the phrase or keys legibly and store them in a safe place.

Chapter II

EXCHANGES

Cryptocurrency exchanges have long been one of the greatest promoters of cryptocurrencies beyond this they are also one of the best platforms to promote new projects

We have three types of exchanges in this space

CENTRALISED EXCHANGES(CEXs)

These are the most commonly used exchanges and they are characterized by simpler and more customer-friendly interfaces. They also have customer service and media outlets that interact with their users.

When looking for an exchange, one thing to look out for is their security history, innovations and user-friendliness.

This kind of exchange manages your assets and you may need a KYC when signing up.

Some of the top 10 exchanges are Binance, FTX, Coinbase, kraken, Kucoin, Bybit, Gate,io, Bitfinix, Huobi Global and Gemini.

Most of the crypto Exchanges offer similar services, such as Spot trading, Futures trading, Margin trading and Staking.

if you haven't used an exchange before you can simply watch some youtube videos on how to use the exchanges, it shouldn't be difficult.

DECENTRALISED EXCHANGES(DEXs)

These kinds of exchanges have no central authority, the trades here are automated and carried out by smart contracts. You do not need KYC when signing up and there is no customer service. On Dexs you have the security keys and actually own your tokens on the blockchain. They are more secure and may not be as user-friendly as the CEXs.

Examples of DEXs are: Uniswap, pancakeswap, dydx and 1inch.

HYBRID EXCHANGES (HEXs)

This is a combination of DEx and CEx, here users can decide to hold their keys.

HEXs tries to build on the things that are not available in both exchanges if they stand independently. HEXs try to reduce the High trading fees in DEXs.

Examples of Hybrid exchanges are: Mt. Gox, BitFloor, and Poloniex

SPOT TRADING

Before we go into trading you need to understand a few terms that will be often used in this space.

SL: STOP LOSS this is the price you want the trade to close if the trade Is going against your prediction.

TP: TAKE PROFIT: This is the price you are willing to exit the market with a profit.

SPOT TRADING

Spot trading is the most common trading option used by all. Spot trading buys or sells an asset at the current price or a specified price with regard to your stipulated amount. Spot trading relies on your budget.

Limit Order

A limit order requires you to fill the price you want to buy or sell at, the amount or worth of the asset you want to buy.

When the price gets to your stipulated price a sell or buy is triggered as you chose.

Market Order

A market buy or sell is an instant order. This tells the system to sell or buy at any available price, this is usually what I call panic selling or buying and this is never advisable.

People who do market trades just want to get in or get out of the trade at any price this could be Fear Of Missing Out (FOMO) or fear of losing all.

Stop Limit Order

A stop-limit order combines a stop trigger and a limit order. Stop-limit orders allow traders to set the minimum amount of profit they're happy to take or the maximum they're willing to spend or lose on a trade

Buy Stop Limit Order

This actually acts as a trigger to place a limit order, you may want to refer to the explanation I gave for the limit order above.

Assuming you want to buy BTC but the price is at 29400, and you have done your analysis and feel that if BTC gets to 29600 that it will surely pump, you can use the buy limit, saying that if BTC crosses 29600 buy for me at 29650.

Why you are buying higher is so that you will not miss out on the trade, therefore offering higher than the current price at that time so that your order can be filled.

Sell Stop Limit

This works the same way as the Buy Stop limit but this time on the downwards trend. let's say you are already in a trade and you fill there will be a sharp downwards trend you can use a sell stop limit as follows.

For example, you bought BTC at 29600 and after your analysis, you feal that BTC will go down to 29200 but instead of waiting for that, you use a sell-stop limit. Now if the price touches 29400 the system should sell at 29300, with this you will not incur too much loses.

Trailing Stop

This is akin to a stop limit, this follows your position using a pre-determined percentage movement.

For example, if you are in a trade and making profit, but you don't want to exit yet, because you feel you can get more out of the market, using a trailing stop will allow you to put a percentage difference in the case of market volatility. If you bought the coin at 0.4$ and the price rose up to 0.45$ showing that you are in profit, you can use a trailing stop and put a percentage you can accommodate when the market moves against you or for you.

So your stop loss continues to move upwards as the price of the asset moves up and if the asset falls by the percentage you put, the trade will close and vice versa.

So if you have a 5% trailing stop and the current price of the asset is 4$, and your Take profit is 4.5$ with a Trailing profit of 10% if the price moves to 6.5$ your stop loss will move to 5.5$ so if there is a downward movement the system will close your trade at 5.5.

OCO

This simply means one cancels the other, this type of trade allows you to put your limit buy, then a stop limit price.
Assuming an asset is trading between 4$ - 5$ with OCO you can create an order that buys below 4$ or above 5$ so an OCO helps you to create 2 limit others and a stop limit order.

For example, if an asset is trading between 4 - 5$ you can put your price at 5$ and stop at 4$ and limit at 4.2$. Meaning my target price to buy is 5$ but if the asset price returns to 4$ buy for me at 4.2$. This can also be used in sell Trade or even a trade you are already in.

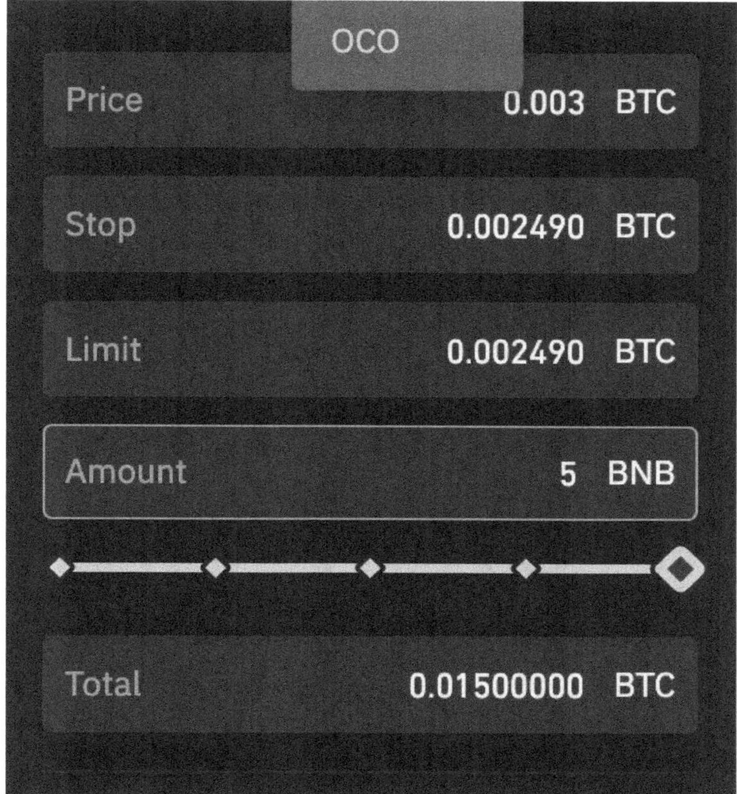

FUTURES TRADING

This is the fastest way to lose money and maybe make money too. I personally do not trade futures as much as I trade Spot.

Futures trading doesn't require traders to actually hold the asset but buy or sell derivatives.

The most profitable part of this is the leverage you can use. Traders can use leverage to increase their positions, making more gains or losses, either way, the price goes.

Trading Futures is fun when you are making gains, I usually don't advise anyone to go above 5X leverage as I do not take crypto trading as a get-rich-quick game, but as a lasting profession.

Some of the advantages of trading futures are, Leveraging, High liquidity, low trading fees, short selling and most significant trading volume.

The futures trading sections also allowS you to use the instruments such as Market Order, Limit Order and OCO Trades.

Trading Futures is a serious business and should be done with caution, having proper risk management, Stop-Loss and Take profit is a must.

Sticking to the plan or developing a trading method is germane to your success in trading futures.

I will refer you to the *one-trade-a-day* trading techniques to assist in creating your technique for futures trading.

One of the things to note in futures trading is to try to save your gains, as one of the problems traders face is losing the money they made especially when using leverage, things can easily go south.

In trading futures discipline is very important, Stop loss and Take profit must be applied at all times.

P2P

P2P Simply means peer-to-peer and this is the fastest way to get into the crypto space for countries whose banks are not in support of crypto transactions.

There are a lot of P2P marketplaces out there but the most used is the Binance p2p market.

If you would like to learn how to use a p2p market place do well to check out some videos on youtube for that, but here I am going to explain what to look out for or avoid while using a p2p marketplace.

Always refresh the page before doing any transaction to make sure all the prices are updated.

look for people with at least 90% success rate this is important because the rating is not fancy, it actually shows how many times this person has done a successful transaction.

When you select the person that meets your requirement make sure to again refresh the peer's page.

Make sure you are putting the right details and Bank accounts always cross-check.

Never approve payment if anything goes wrong along the line.

Always check your bank App to make sure you received the fund before approving your transaction.

If you are buying, chat with the person before making payment to make sure they are online.

Chapter III

GETTING STARTED RIGHT

One thing I would like to do is to manage your expectations so that we can succeed together. Your ability to make a profit after reading this E-book adds to the success of this book. But more important is your ability to stay long enough in this space to build yourself and show the light to others.

To start trading requires capital and in the following lessons, we will be experimenting with 100$ and trading the Spot market.

For those with more capital, that will also be welcomed but remember my No1 rule, do not trade with money you need for daily things like groceries and transportation to work, or school fees or child support, do not gamble make a plan for this as an investment.

You can use the P2P market to buy some stablecoins that will give you access to other cryptocurrencies. The crypto market runs 24/7,

Sunday to Saturday.

It is always advisable to start small and reinvest your gains instead of putting in more money because *whatever goes up must surely come down.*

There are three major types of traders:

Scalping

These traders trade for minutes or a few hours, they usually have a target and when they reach that target they close the market for the day, and when they don't, they still leave within their apportioned time for trading. They are strategic traders who know what they want from the market and if they are not getting it they close.

Day traders

This kind of traders do not let their trades go over to the next day, they close their trades as the market closes. Though the crypto market doesn't officially close, they close their trades on or before 11:50 pm. They take their profits or cut their losses.

Swing Traders

Swing traders leave their trades for a little longer, days and even weeks, this type of trader is patient and follows the market until they are in profit.

This is generally the most used trading method.

Position Traders

These guys serve as investors in the space, they are long-term traders, and they can hold a position for months or even years. They are not worried about the little movements but have a clear idea of the long-term direction of tokens.

ICO AND HYPES

ICO simply means Initial Coin Offering, A way by which new projects and startups raise funds for the development of their platforms.

ICO is widely used in the crypto space to get tokens into the hands of trades at a very early stage of the project, the reward of investing at this time is that you get the token at a very cheap price and some projects never return to their ICO prices.

ICO trading is not an easy fit as many ICO are done by criminals who just want to take your money and zoom off, that is why the platform that is selling the ICO is very important.
The majority of the ICO I bought that actually did well was bought on Coinlist.

Here I will detail the steps on how to get on coinlist.

- Signup on coinlist and put your ID
- Make sure you have an international passport for some African countries.

- Send some USDT or USDC to the wallet in preparation.
- Read the information about the token you want to buy
- Answer the Q&A
- Make sure you arrive early to the token sales.
- Do not use a VPN
- Do not sign in to one account on more than one device.
- Make sure you complete your payment, if not you will be penalized.

There are other listing platforms but Coinlist has over time proved to be more fruitful. Buying a token during its ICO serves you a great advantage and you should try getting in.

When getting into an ICO on coinlist you should think long-term as most of them will be locked up for a year or more.
So many platforms have used hype and celebrities to sell their projects without actually having value for people's money and time. Hyping a project is one thing that has become the order of the day for gullible people and the majority of newbies.

If you truly understand the fundamentals of a good project and the values it should be built on you will understand that Hyping is for get-rich-quick projects that never last.

A project is valued by the services it has to offer not by how many people are singing its praises.

PUMP AND DUMP

This is a common term known in the crypto space for bad projects or projects with low Volume that is most times used by greedy people to deceive others.

Pump and Dump projects are known for their low volume which attracts bad actors to manipulate the prices.

One of the worst things to do is to join a pump and dump group, they will surely scam you.

Pump and dump groups try to gather enough people to believe they will make something happen. But they have their VIP traders who choose these low-volume coins, so they and their friends buy the token at least a few minutes before the token is announced, when it is announced the token must have done 50% already and they start cashing out.

Pump and dump groups have ruined many people's money and you should refrain from it, by all means, they are very unhealthy.
All you need do is just follow some good crypto buddies on Twitter and youtube, some very good groups that are information based on telegram too, that's all you need.

Anything that is too good to be true in this space is a scam.

Be careful of MLM structures marketing strategies, they ask you to bring people to earn, be careful of such.

No trader or person can give you an absolute amount on a monthly basis because nothing is 100% sure in this space. Don't give people to trade for you, trade for yourself and bear the risk.

Web3

Web 3 is the next level of the web, users can now make an impact and actually own part of the development of the web

From 1999 - 2004 we have been using web 1, which was the read-only web, here users were not allowed to make changes on the web and they were not interactive.

Web 1 was just a read-only website of companies and information.

Web 2 which started in 2004 brought in interaction and participation. Big companies like Facebook, Twitter and the likes allowed users to be part of creating content and interaction between users was another feature of web2. Web2 which is what is currently used now has some limitations that have led to the invention of web3.

Web3 solves a lot of issues that web 2 has, as web 3 is the decentralised version of web 2, web3 allows users to own part of the web in form of tokens and NFT. Payment is swift as people are connected with their crypto wallets which allows intercontinental transactions.

Web3 rewards creators and is trustless thereby removing the need for central trusted authorities like the banks or governments.

Web3 is permission-less it is not restricted, anyone anywhere can access it using the internet.

Current Limitations of Web3

As fun as web3 sounds, there are still a lot of improvements to be made on it as it is still work in process.

Education

This is one of the key factors affecting web3 for now, as many people lack the understanding of the use of web3 and how it betters their web experience.

Infrastructure

Web3 is heavily dependent on web2 Apps and centralized organization as it is still young and growing.

Cost

Web3 will be ideal for richer communities and does not solve the issue of high transaction fees.

Non Fungible Tokens (NFT)

2021 was the year of NFT, GameFi and a lot of DFi projects. What really is NFT and how do they get their values?

Pictures, Video, Audio, Photographs anything at all can be stored on the blockchain. Fungible stands for anything that one part or quantity can be replaced by another part or quantity. So Non-Fungible tokens are tokens that can't be replaced by another.

The value of these tokens is perceived value and may not conform to demand and supply.

The value of NFT is dependent on the community, characteristics, rarity and use cases as well.

The uses of NFT

Ensuring the Authenticity of Products is one way NFT can be used, as the information about a product can be stored on the blockchain. With NFT the information of the last buyer of a product can be seen and the generation of the NFT can also be part of the authenticity check if stored on the blockchain.

NFT can be used in real estate for proof of ownership and other documents that authentication is required.

ID cards can be a form of NFT, that is minted on the blockchain, with this information, the user can be stored and easily verified.

Metaverse is another place NFT is playing a great role, as these NFT can be bought and sold in metaverse games and social Apps.

NFT can be used to authenticate Artworks and many more.

The business of NFT is dependent on the community and the story behind the NFT. The biggest market for NFT is Opensea, you can find most projects there and they dominate the NFT market.

Buying an NFT doesn't assure you to make money as there are so many scams in the market. People mint and resell the same NFT to make others feel its has value. The NFT space has been so bastardized it is very hard to find real value in it.

Chapter IV

CALCULATING ENTRY

One of my strategies is to always have a good entry, it is as if you are bargaining for a product so getting it at a good price is a priority.

Having a good entry helps you meet your target quicker and reduces your chances of losing money, remember not losing money is gain

It is always good to have a target profit for a trade, aim for 2 -5% per trade depending on your capital.

Assuming you want to gain 2% from the market in the trade, you should set your entry price 1% lower from the current price or at the support.

Let your budget = 100$

price of token = 4$

Target gain = 2% of 100$ = 2$

Number of tokens you will get = 25 @ 4$ for 100$

Your target price = 2% of 4$ = 0.08

Now to get your entry we will divide the 0.8 by 2 =0.04

Entry will 4 - 0.04 = 3.96

Exit price = 4 + 0.04 = 4.04

So between 3.96 - 4.04, you will get 0.08 which is the % that will fetch you 2% of your 100$

Learning how to do entries like this can be very useful in a less volatile market, but then if the market is volatile you should use Support and resistance.

Support and resistance have long been used as entry and exit points for long, we are going to look at what this means.

SUPPORT

To explain this as simple as possible, support is the price or point where the price of an asset bounces back up.

The best range to measure support is on the 4hrs time frame, at that price where there is a change in the direction of the price movement is the support. Support means a wedge to prevent the price from falling lower.

To note the point as shown in the figure above, you will see a bounce off many times on that level or price. You must ensure more than two or more support on a straight line before using it as your support.

Support can be broken, but if support is created and has been held repeatedly, then that becomes strong support and the price will assuredly retest or re-touch that zone again.

Most traders enter their trades here

RESISTANCE

This is the level on the upside that the tokens price has reached and repeatedly dropped from there.

So resistance stands as a wedge preventing the upwards movement of the price, This price is where most traders exit their trade.

Resistance is established after the weak, or candle touched this particular level and goes down repeatedly. This level must be tested at least twice to confirm that it is a resistance using the 4-hour time frame.

FINDING THE RIGHT PROJECT

If you have a strong enough why, HOW, will not be a problem.

Subscribing to the right project is very important and the next few lectures will deliberate on that. You must have favourite projects, projects that you have been monitoring for some time and understand their behaviour.

Projects have different communities, team builders and technology so they can't be treated the same way, I strongly suggest that you pen down the projects you are interested in and start watching their behaviour and how they act when BTC is going up or down.

As we all are aware that BTC is the king of the market and BTC always pumps first and others follow, but after that, some coins still behave differently and there are some coins that even pump while BTC is pumping or dumping.

What to look out for in finding your favourite projects.

1. The technology must be new and ever-improving, the technology must be evolving with the trend.

2. The project must have a good communication system that seriously sends out information about what they are doing.

3. The team must have good knowledge of Cryptocurrency and a background in the space.

4 The project must be community driven

5. Preferably look for projects below 1$

6. Check how they behave towards BTC.

Write down these projects at least 10 projects and start to monitor them closely.

MARKET CIRCLES

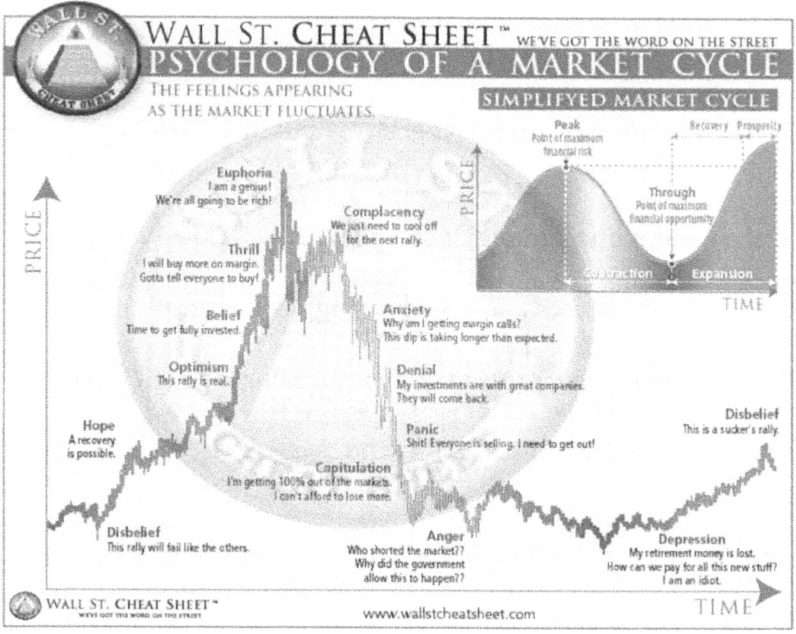

The circle the crypto market goes is significant and is unending from the picture above you can tell which point we are in and how to act accordingly.

The biggest losses people encounter in the market is by not sticking to the most important rule.

Buy low and sell High, as simple as this sounds, *things that are simple to do are always simple not to do too.*

People consistently buy High and sell low out of **FOMO** or **FUED.**

The need to maintain a strategy and follow it judiciously is very important for your success. People buy high because of *FOMO(Fear Of Missing Out)* they wait for people to tell them when to buy instead of doing their own research.

The truth of the matter is that when you start hearing about a project from everyone, then it is time to exit.

This circle has some important stages we will discuss.

Accumulation Stage

The point where people lose hope and sell off is the time people start buying, this is the period where everything has flattened out and the people have lost hope in the trade, that is when good traders and institutions start buying. Here you can see the range, it goes up in the morning and dips at night, goes down during the weekdays and goes up during the weekends. There is no major movement at this point.

The Markup Stage

At this point, the market is stabilizing and you can see upwards movement. Here the greens are coming in steadily and those that are good in analysis are coming in as well. Here people are still buying and some people are exiting the market as well so there is a battle between sellers and buyers.

Distribution Stage

This stage is where the sellers come in, those that bought at the accumulation stage start selling. You start to hear people make 10X and make a lot of noises about their winnings. This is where the newbies come in because they have heard a thing or two about cryptocurrency.

This Stage can take months and people are generally greedy at this point.

The Markdown Stage

This is the stage that seems like the end of the world, everything is falling and those who bought at the distribution stage are not happy at this time. Usually, newbies are the ones caught up in this stage and long-time holders. Day traders and swing traders are already out of the market for long. This is the time newbies try to cut their Loses and just further below is another circle.

When you use the cheat sheet, you should be able to identify what point you are in and how to act accordingly.

Warren Buffett: Be Fearful When Others Are Greedy

Chapter V

FUNDAMENTAL ANALYSIS

Evaluating an asset for investment decisions has always been the most important thing to do in crypto trading, understanding the way to evaluate a coin helps you make the right choice for your money.

In this lecture, I am going to explain how to evaluate tokens but surely the decision to invest in crypto is totally yours as I have mentioned before it is risky and human beings are unpredictable.

There are two major ways to analyse the value or movement of a token. one is the fundamental analysis, which focuses on the information, rumours, Publications, whitepapers and functionality of the project.

Whitepaper

The whitepaper is a document published by the developers of a project to interest you on what the project is all about, how the team has planned to execute the project, how the token is to be shared and used, and what the project aims to accomplish.

Reading the white paper is most times neglected by traders but if you want to know about a project at least hear from the creators of the project first.

When reading a whitepaper concentrate on the under-listed topics

Token Model

This looks into the amount of token that is minted, deflationary meaning does the token reduce in quantity as people get hold of it, a deflationary token has a limited amount that can be minted and increases in value as more people buy the token because of the idea of a limited supply.I f the token is inflationary meaning the token can increase in supply.

Token Distribution.

This refers to how the token is being dished out to the public, the information here gives traders an idea if the token can be mined, earned, owned and about the governing community.

Token Supply.

This looks into the number of tokens minted, the circulating supply and the maximum supply.

Technical Subtleties of the project.

This section talks about the technology used in building the token, the protocol and the mechanism.

Team

The team of every project is more important than the project because without capable hands you will lose your money.

You must check if they are involved in other projects that have failed and what made them switch, you must also be aware of Ponzi schemes and offers that are too good to be true.

News and Publications

It is important to follow the news and publications of a project you want to trade, check what people are saying about it and if they have been in the news recently.

Every project from time to time puts out publications to let the public know about the recent developments of the project and simple updates, this information helps you figure out if the project is alive and that is what people majorly trade with.

Sites like Cointelegraph.com and a lot of them are out there.

Community

The community of a project is the driving force and the lifeline of the project, an active community shares information about the project and gets more people into the project, and the marketing and communications of the project must be able to deliver on this.

The role of an active community cannot be over emphasized as this is where the hype happens. Studies have shown that hype sells more than projects with good fundamentals as people will listen to who is talking about a project that what the project has to offer.

Many of these projects have their communities on telegram and should be easy to access.

Utility

What value does the project bring to the ecosystem, what problem is it solving, and does the project have use cases, which can make it desirable even if the price doesn't go up? Is there a need for the token apart from speculations?

Social Media

Social media is another avenue where project promote their products and this helps it spread faster as people start to make gains, the community starts promoting the project even if the project will end soon.

When you start seeing a lot of wins on a particular project, know that the end is near, as, after this kind of bull runs, tokens without worth always come crashing, but surely this is an avenue to learn more about a project, also follow knowledgeable people in the crypto space, follow crypto conversation on Twitter and youtube as well.

Vision and Culture

Projects that have vision or purpose most times do well because they tend to build believers, who become die-hard fans of the project and these people usually don't sell out the project. So one must be careful to note these projects that have a vision that is relatable and that empowers humanity.

Environmental Factors

Some other factors that play a significant role in the market are environmental factors. Many people don't talk about this but undoubtedly the Environment affects the market in a significant way.

Truly when you are trading in the crypto market you are already playing in the world economy but truth be told the world is a global community, and we affect each other.

Natural Disaster is something that adversely affects the world economy and when one set of people are suffering the country's economy feels it and that will reflect on how many people are putting money into crypto projects or removing money from them.

So one needs to be current and up to date on global news if one wants to be a good trader.

World Economy

Environmental factors affect the economy of countries, likewise bad leadership, corruption and bad management. When things happen on a national level it affects the crypto space whether good or bad.

Like the corona pandemic affected the market, I will say positively as within this time the US government was handing cash to citizens and those citizens put a lot in crypto and we could see the uptrend during the lockdown period.

In the 2nd quarter of 2023, we saw inflation all over, and wars, this as well affected the market as central banks offered more interest on deposits, people saved more and that affected the crypto market as well.

Bans and Sanctions

When countries ban cryptocurrency it always has an effect on the market and in most cases triggers a sell-off, Sometimes countries ban mining and the resources that the miners had used to build their rigs go to waste, this kind of sanctions and Bans affect the market too.

Whenever China bans crypto the market always sells off and bounces back later. Also, watch out for big companies and entities that influence the market.

TECHNICAL ANALYSIS

This is basically Analyzing the future price of assets based on previous behavior. Technical analysts are of the opinion that history repeats itself. Technical analysis however should not be used alone but should be used with some fundamental information about the project.

There are so many instruments one can use in technical analysis but we are tailoring this to the most important ones or basically the most used ones.

Candlestick Chart

Learning to use the candlestick chart pattern will be the 1st of many you need to learn, as this is the basic, understanding of what the candle stick represents.

The candlesticks tells a story in every time frame, the battle between the bulls and the bears. It shows what is happening in the market between the bulls and the bears. I prefer to use the Heikin Ashi candles they have better representation.

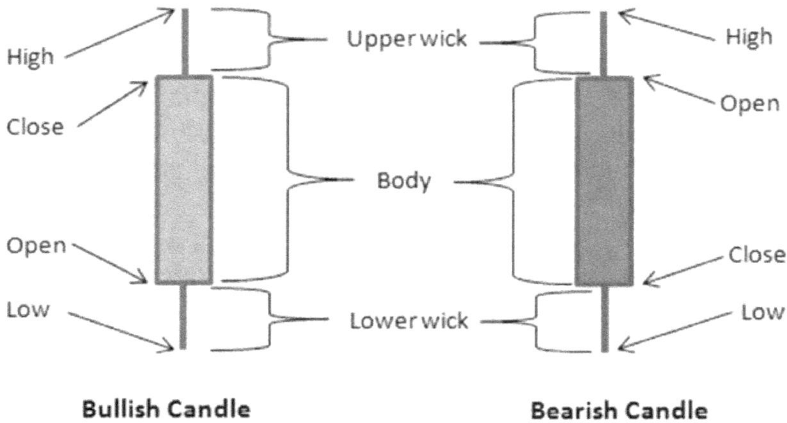

The candle story is about a tug of war between buyers and sellers at a particular time frame. Using the green candle for example is regarded as a bullish candle, kindly examine the picture above for a better understanding. The **open** on the picture above is where the buyers came in but the sellers were strong and pushed the price lower to the section where the arrow points to **Low**, then the bulls or buyers took over again and pushed the price to the peak labeled as **High**, then some bears came in again at that point pulled it down (sold) to the close and that is how the candle ends.

The same goes for the red candle also called the bearish candle. The story can be interpreted as follows, the bearish candle started at the **Open** as indicated by the arrow, buyers took over at bought some which took it to the **High**, sellers came back and sold it down to the **Low**, and buyers came in again and bought the market up to the **Close**

The bearish candle always opens at the top while the Bullish

candle starts from the bottom. This is a continuous story that tells you who is winning in every time frame and can help you make some decisions about the trend of a project.

The candles create the trend, continuous bullish candles means an up trend and that the bulls have taken over but the bearish market is characterized by the candle's continuous lower lows. Do well to study the candle stick picture above.

Support and Resistance

This topic has been treated before as a way to find the hedge for both the upside trend and downside trend. Please see page 18

Moving Average

The moving average is used to determine the price direction based on past prices. The moving average gives you the average price of the asset. The longer the period for the moving average, the greater the lag. We have 20-day, 50-day and 200-day moving averages. The whole idea of a moving average is to tell you the direction of the asset and trend. No technical instrument can stand alone to help you make a market decision as I have always said, The market tells the behaviours of human beings and they are not all based on past performance.

Relative Strength Index (RSI)

RSI measures the speed and magnitude of an assets recent price changes. This helps to point out when the asset is overvalued or undervalued.

During an uptrend for any time frame, an oversold reading is when the line goes below 30 and for a downtrend, an over-bought will be when the line crosses 50.

One thing about RSI is that to effectively use it, you must understand the trend and as I always say, these instruments are used with other instruments as well.

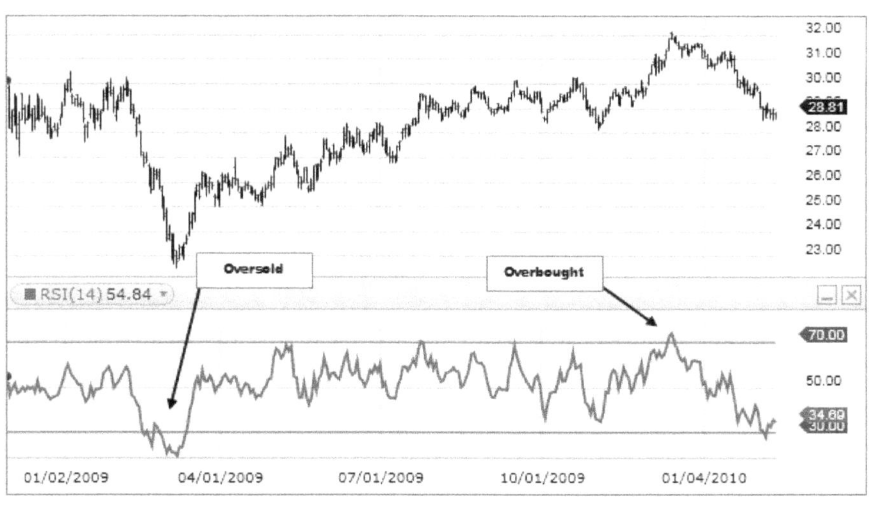

Bollinger Bands

This is another commonly used instrument that helps you to determine overbought or oversold conditions in the market.

The Bollinger Bands usually contain three lines, the lowest, the middle and the top, the candles are plotted within these three line and with it, you can tell if the market is going up or down and even shows the volatility, by the length of the candles and distance between the lines. The Middle line is usually a 20 days period

Movement Average. The Bollinger band always comes in handy to support the RSI.

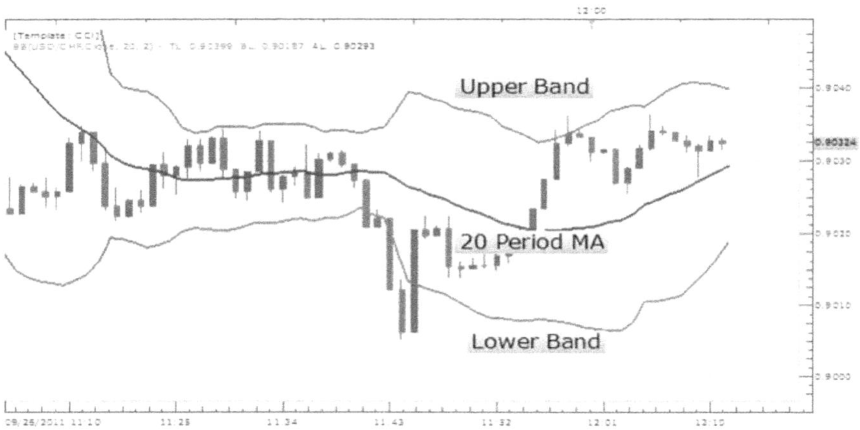

Volume Profile

VP is one of the instruments that I have fallen in love with because this exposes the big traders and institutional traders. The VP shows at what price the highest volume of sells was and at what price the highest volume of buys was, in order words, you can use the VP to back up your Support and Resistance levels. Though the Volume Profile is not a free feature of trading view but if you can get this, it will help a lot.

"Volume profile" indicator shows the buying and selling strength of the stock within a certain time period.
It helps to identify the possible support and resistance levels within a trend.
It also shows the range of price consolidation for the day
MAX
MIN

Chapter VI

ONE TRADE PER DAY

The concept of one trade per day was developed to help you survive in the crypto market during a bearish market and can easily be applied to a bull market too. This concept has been tested and very successful, like I always say *no technique in this space is 100% sure.*

We will be using a lot of tradingview instruments and we will help you familiarize the environment of tradingview to suit our technique.

tradingview.com is the go-to site when doing an analysis, it has numerous instruments that will help you do your research. Using tradingview is not difficult at all if you understand how to trade already or have done a bit of technical analysis on exchanges.

Step1

Finding the right token to trade is not as easy as it seems, one best way is to go to coinmarketcap or coingecko to find the coin people are talking about.

Another way is to go to your exchange and click on the market and find the general trend for the day. If the general trend is bearish, then you go bearish, if the general trend is bullish then you go bullish.

When trading any side, you must make sure you are following the trend and also looking for tokens that are between(+1 to +3 against usdt) this is for the bullish trend, for the bearish trend(-1 to -3) look for a token that falls within that range below the usdt.

Get at least 5 tokens that you are going to be working with for that day.

Step 2

Log on to the website(tradingview.com) look for the search bar and put the name of the token you want to analyse. Select the token against usdt and click on see over view.

When you click overview, click on technicals. Now on the screen, you will have oscillators, summary and Moving Averages, below that are other technical analyses.

if you scroll down the site, you will see other trading instruments and what they are pointing to, at the end of each instrument you will see buy or sell.

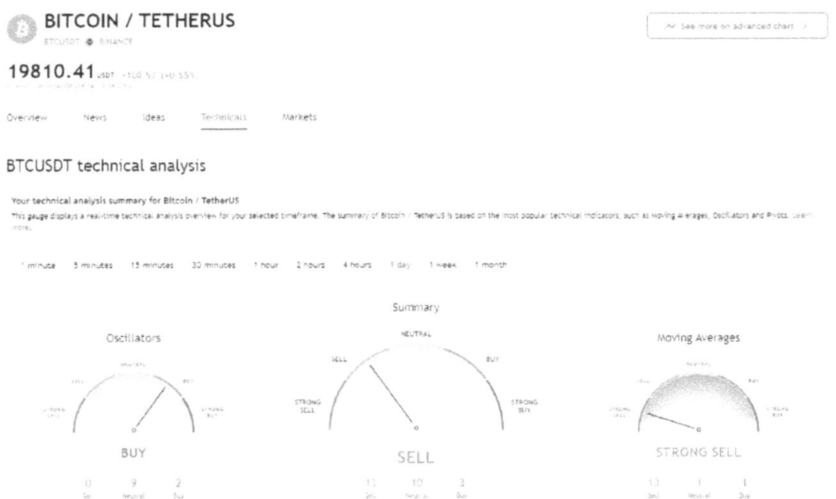

So tradingview has done all the technical analyses that you need to make a decision and so there is no need to do them yourself again.

So if they all point in one direction then you should follow. So what I do is use the time frame on the chart side and see if at all time frame it points to a particular direction.

With this you have a summary of what all the technical analyses is pointing to.

The next thing you need to do is use the entry calculation if you have been following this book to enter your trade or simply use the support to get an entry.

OSCILLATORS ›

Name	Value	Action
Relative Strength Index (14)	43.31	Neutral
Stochastic %K (14, 3, 3)	32.73	Neutral
Commodity Channel Index (20)	-47.07	Neutral
Average Directional Index (14)	21.03	Neutral
Awesome Oscillator	-419.64	Neutral
Momentum (10)	1022.65	Buy
MACD Level (12, 26)	-302.90	Buy
Stochastic RSI Fast (3, 3, 14, 14)	44.04	Neutral
Williams Percent Range (14)	-69.63	Neutral
Bull Bear Power	-1357.92	Neutral
Ultimate Oscillator (7, 14, 28)	46.04	Neutral

MOVING AVERAGES ›

Name	Value	Action
Exponential Moving Average (10)	20376.33	Sell
Simple Moving Average (10)	20575.96	Sell
Exponential Moving Average (20)	20552.88	Sell
Simple Moving Average (20)	20198.28	Sell
Exponential Moving Average (30)	20807.73	Sell
Simple Moving Average (30)	20559.39	Sell
Exponential Moving Average (50)	21353.80	Sell
Simple Moving Average (50)	21758.43	Sell
Exponential Moving Average (100)	23446.70	Sell
Simple Moving Average (100)	21737.17	Sell
Exponential Moving Average (200)	26283.52	Sell
Simple Moving Average (200)	29707.76	Sell
Ichimoku Base Line (9, 26, 52, 26)	20654.88	Neutral
Volume Weighted Moving Average (20)	20309.87	Sell
Hull Moving Average (9)	19650.36	Buy

The world is ever-changing so should you, keep learning and you will soar.

ARBITRAGE TRADING

This is a cool way to make cash from the crypto market by trading across the exchanges that have the same token.

The most beautiful part of this is that it helps to balance the price in the market and it's good for the project.

Finding a coin to arbitrage is key as many of these tokens don't give such opportunities. Tokens that give this opportunity are mostly low-cap coins with low trading activity.

To spot these tokens you need to pay attention to exchanges which you can simply do with coinmarketcap or coingecko.

Doing arbitrage trading requires you to have accounts in the exchanges where the token is listed.

You need to check for liquidity on all the exchanges you want to do the arbitrage this is to ensure that you can sell after buying.

You must check the profit you are making if it is worth the risk you are taking because it is risky too and the market can move at any time.

You must check the cost of transferring the token, which could add extra expenses to you as well.

You must have the capital to make profit from the trade as the larger the trade, the more profit and loss you can make.

Step 1

Find the coin that meets the requirement stated above

Step 2

Buy the coin on the cheapest exchange

Step 3

Send the coin to the exchange where it is more expensive and sell it

Step 4

Send back your money in a stablecoin to the cheaper exchange and repeat the process, each time making sure there is profit to be made before proceeding.

THE THREE STAGE METHOD

This method was actually taught to me by one of my big bosses, this method has proven to be very smart and hence makes it to this book.

If you have read with understanding, you will notice that I am more into saving your gains and not losing money, which is something that is very important. Making money is hard, but losing money is so easy here.

The 3 stage method tells you to always divide your trades into 3 either sell or buy trades.

For example, if you are trading with 300$ and you are about to enter a trade, it is advisable you enter the trade with 100$, if the trade goes against your prediction, you add an extra 100$, and if it continues downwards to a price you feel this is a lucky price or extreme conditions then you can use the remaining 100$.

This process will average your loss and makes it more bearable. If the trade goes towards your prediction, put another 100$ at the initial price you bought.

When you are selling too, divide it into three, sell at the top and wait, if it continues upwards, look for milestones and sell at such points.

For example:

Trading Budget = 300$, your preferred entry point is 0.004$

Buy 100$ at that price (this secures your position so you don't miss out totally)

If the price goes lower to 0.038$ you can put the second 100$

If the price goes to let's say 0.003 you can now buy the last 100$

What if the Price starts going upward then put another buy at your 1st entry

when you are in profit, you should divide the trade into 3 too, you can sell 100$ at 0.0045$

Then at 0.0047$ you can sell the second 100$

The last is meant for the peak.

You should be able to get the idea at this point.

Chapter VII

BUILDING YOUR CRYPTO PROFILE

In most things we learn, there are two ways to earn, one by doing it and the other by teaching it. You can do either or both.

Building your crypto profile means identifying with your crypto buddies and showing off your skills in the space.

The best way to learn is to teach, but in this space, you may need proof, Proof of knowledge which tells people that you actually understand by your earnings in crypto.

The first step to presenting yourself is to build a good outlook, on social media channels, it is advisable you separate your online crypto self from your everyday self, this helps you to distinguish which post goes to what place.

Channels you must have

- Twitter
- Telegram
- Tiktok
- Youtube

Your Twitter or any social media channel must have a good profile photo of you and any picture with the background showing you in the midst of friends in any event or crypto setting.

You should follow important people in the space and follow projects that interest you.

The second step is to share your knowledge, do your research and start putting your knowledge out there, you can start from whatever information you have, even those you think everyone knows.

Steadily interact with your audience and join other people's live videos and ask questions.

Be humble so that you can get help easily to achieve your aim.

Join Telegram communities and be active, offer help where you can, and be consistent.

Post crypto-related topics on crypto groups and your status.

Be up to date in information and do your research always.

About the Author

Austin Amadi is a crypto enthusiast who started his career as a marketing executive and has a lot of experience in Traditional Marketing, Digital Marketing, Blockchain Marketing, Graphic Design and Technology. He has experience in Forex trading and Crypto Trading. He has been trading in the financial Market for seven years.

Austin Amadi has worked with Crypto exchanges, Cryptocurrency start-ups and is currently a business development analyst for a blockchain company.

www.ingramcontent.com/pod-product-compliance
Lightning Source LLC
LaVergne TN
LVHW050330160826
845677LV00014B/3575